# BUILDING A
# GAMING PC 2025

The Ultimate Guide to Building, Upgrading, and
Optimizing Your Gaming Rig with the Latest Hardware
and Trends for Peak Performance

Robert I. Grass

# Disclaimer

The content in this guide is for informational purposes only. While every effort has been made to ensure the accuracy of the information, the author and publisher make no guarantees about its reliability or suitability for your specific needs.

By using this guide, you agree that the author is not responsible for any damages, losses, or issues that may arise from following the steps or recommendations outlined. If you are uncertain about any aspect of building a gaming PC, it is advised to seek professional assistance.

# Preface

The quality of your gaming experience is largely determined by the performance and power of your gaming computer. Whether you're a dedicated gamer aiming to construct the ultimate custom-built rig, a casual player seeking a smoother and more responsive gaming experience, or a competitive gamer striving for ultra-fast performance, knowing how to properly build, upgrade, and fine-tune your gaming PC is crucial. This guide has been specifically designed to serve as a comprehensive resource for anyone eager to enhance their gaming setup and take full advantage of the latest advancements in gaming technology throughout 2025 and beyond.

# Table of Contents

**Preface**......................................................... **4**

**Introduction to the Gaming Landscape**....... **9**

How This Guide Will Enhance Your Gaming Experience........................................................ 13

**Chapter 1: Understanding Gaming Computers** .............................................. **17**

The Evolution of Gaming PCs ............................ 17

Key Components and Their Roles ...................... 22

Assessing Your Gaming Needs ..........................28

**Chapter 2: Planning Your Gaming Rig** ...... **34**

Setting a Budget: Finding the Perfect Balance Between Cost and Performance ......................... 35

Defining Your Gaming Goals and Preferences...43

Researching and Ensuring Component Compatibility......................................................40

**Chapter 3: Essential Components for a High-Performance Gaming PC**.......................... **43**

Central Processing Unit (CPU): The Heart of System Performance.................................................50

Graphics Processing Unit (GPU): The Key to Stunning Visuals.................................................53

Motherboard: The Foundation of Your Gaming Rig .................................................................55

Memory (RAM): Speed and Efficiency for Gaming .................................................................56

Storage: Faster Load Times for Seamless Gaming .................................................................57

Power Supply Unit (PSU): Reliable Power for Stability .................................................................58

Cooling Systems .................................................................59

**Chapter 4: Building Your Gaming PC........ 62**

Preparing Your Workspace .................................................63

Step-by-Step Assembly Guide ...........................................65

First Boot and BIOS Configuration ....................................70

Installing the Operating System..........................................72

**Chapter 5: Optimizing Your Gaming Rig....79**

Updating Drivers and Firmware ...................... 80

Overclocking for Enhanced Performance .........83

Configuring Game Settings for Optimal
Performance ......................................................85

Utilizing Performance Monitoring Tools ..........87

**Chapter 6: Advanced Enhancements......... 90**

Customizing Your PC Case for Aesthetics and
Functionality ...................................................... 91

Implementing Advanced Cooling Solutions for
Optimal Performance .......................................94

Setting Up Multi-GPU Configurations: Are They
Still Worth It? ...................................................96

Virtual Reality (VR) and Ray Tracing
Technologies: The Future of Gaming ................98

**Chapter 7: Troubleshooting and Maintenance**
**........................................................................102**

Diagnosing Common Gaming PC Issues .......... 103

Routine Maintenance for Optimal Performance
........................................................................109

Upgrading Components for Future-Proofing... 110

## Chapter 8: Gaming Peripherals and Accessories ............................................... 113

Choosing the Ideal Gaming Monitor .................113

Gaming Keyboards and Mice: Essential Features ....................................................................118

Audio Solutions: Headsets vs. Speakers............121

Additional Gaming Accessories........................ 122

## Chapter 9: Staying Informed and Connected ........................................................... 125

Engaging with the Gaming Community ........... 126

Keeping Up with Industry Trends.....................131

Resources for Continuous Learning in Gaming 135

## Additional Tips ........................................138

## Appendices ...............................................152

# System Component

## System Component

# Introduction to the Gaming Landscape

Over the past decade, the gaming industry has experienced remarkable transformations. Technological advancements have propelled video games into new realms, offering experiences once deemed unattainable. The integration of virtual reality (VR), augmented reality (AR), and ray tracing has revolutionized player interaction, delivering unprecedented realism and immersion. As we enter 2025, these innovations have become integral to modern gaming, demanding more robust and efficient hardware to keep pace with evolving software requirements.

**In 2025,** gaming computers have evolved to become faster, more compact, and energy-efficient. These advancements provide gamers with immersive experiences characterized by lifelike graphics, swift load times, and enhanced gameplay features. High-performance gaming PCs are now accessible to a broader audience, transcending the realm of professional eSports players and dedicated enthusiasts. A well-optimized system has become essential for any gamer seeking to elevate their gaming experience.

This guide is tailored for individuals aiming to comprehend, build, or upgrade their gaming systems. Whether you're a novice or a seasoned gamer, you'll find practical advice, step-by-step instructions, and up-to-date information on selecting the best components for gaming. From understanding the contribution of each part of your gaming rig to overall performance, to detailed guidance on assembling and maintaining your PC, this book equips you with the knowledge to create a system that operates at its peak.

## How This Guide Will Enhance Your Gaming Experience

The objective of this book is to provide you with comprehensive insights to either build or upgrade your gaming computer in 2025. Here's what you can anticipate:

- **In-Depth Component Analysis:** Gain a thorough understanding of each key component in your gaming PC, including the CPU, GPU, motherboard, and storage devices, and their impact on overall performance.
- **Detailed Assembly Instructions:** Follow a step-by-step guide through the entire process of building a gaming computer, from selecting compatible parts to proper assembly techniques.
- **Performance Optimization Strategies:** Learn how to fine-tune your system for optimal gaming performance, covering aspects like

overclocking, game configuration, and system settings adjustments.

- **Troubleshooting and Maintenance Tips:** Discover effective troubleshooting methods and maintenance practices to ensure your gaming rig operates smoothly over time.

- **Future-Proofing Techniques:** Understand how to select components that will remain relevant with upcoming game releases and technological advancements, ensuring longevity for your setup.

Equipped with the insights from this guide, you'll be empowered not only to design and build a top-tier gaming system but also to navigate the rapidly evolving landscape of gaming technology with confidence. As new advancements emerge, your foundational knowledge will enable you to make savvy, informed decisions, ensuring your gaming rig remains at the cutting edge.

Embarking on this journey into the realm of gaming computers is both thrilling and rewarding. Each component plays a pivotal role in crafting an immersive and seamless gaming experience. In the forthcoming chapters, we'll delve deeply into the essential elements that constitute a gaming computer. You'll gain a comprehensive understanding of how these components interact synergistically, and why each is crucial for attaining optimal gaming performance.

We'll explore the intricacies of central processing units (CPUs), graphics processing units (GPUs), memory (RAM), storage solutions, motherboards, power supplies, and cooling systems. By examining their functions, compatibilities, and the latest innovations, you'll be well-prepared to assemble a gaming rig tailored to your specific preferences and performance requirements.

So, are you ready to embark on this exciting endeavor? Let's dive in and meticulously construct the ultimate gaming machine, ensuring each component is thoughtfully selected and expertly integrated to deliver unparalleled gaming experiences.

# Chapter 1: Understanding Gaming Computers

The quality of your gaming experience is intrinsically linked to the performance and capabilities of your computer. Gaming PCs are meticulously engineered to meet the rigorous demands of contemporary video games, encompassing high-resolution graphics, intricate physics simulations, and sophisticated artificial intelligence. This chapter delves into the evolution of gaming PCs, examines their fundamental components, and offers guidance on evaluating your personal gaming requirements.

## The Evolution of Gaming PCs

The trajectory of gaming computers has closely followed the rapid advancements in video game technology. Initially, early video games operated on basic personal computers (PCs). However, as games evolved to feature enhanced graphics, faster processing needs, and increased memory demands, PCs underwent significant transformations to keep pace.

## The Early Years: 1980s to Early 2000s

During the 1980s, gaming was relatively straightforward. Computers like the Commodore 64 and consoles such as the Atari 2600 were capable of running simple games with limited graphical fidelity. The late '80s and early '90s marked a pivotal shift with the introduction of more powerful graphics cards and accelerated processors. This period saw the emergence of intricate games featuring 3D-rendered environments, necessitating enhanced computing power.

By the late 1990s and early 2000s, gaming PCs began to feature dedicated graphics processing units (GPUs). These GPUs enabled the rendering of 3D graphics essential for immersive gaming experiences. Companies like Nvidia and ATI (now AMD) produced add-on cards that significantly boosted graphical capabilities, allowing for more complex visual elements in games. Notably, Nvidia's introduction of the GeForce 256 in 1999 marked a significant milestone in GPU development.

## The Rise of High-Performance Hardware: Mid-2000s to 2010s

**The mid-2000s** witnessed substantial advancements in gaming PC performance, driven by innovations in both central processing units (CPUs) and GPUs. The release of Nvidia's GeForce 8800 GTX in 2006 represented a significant leap in graphical fidelity, introducing support for DirectX 10 and a unified shader architecture. This advancement paved the way for increasingly powerful GPUs in subsequent years.

As games became more realistic, the demand for faster processors and increased memory intensified.

Quad-core processors and faster RAM became standard among serious gamers, facilitating high-settings gameplay with smooth performance. Additionally, storage solutions evolved, with solid-state drives (SSDs) replacing traditional hard disk drives (HDDs), resulting in faster load times and improved overall system performance.

## The Present and Future: 2025 and Beyond

**By 2025,** gaming PCs have achieved unprecedented sophistication, propelled by technological breakthroughs in graphics, processing power, and system efficiency. Graphics cards, such as Nvidia's RTX 50 series, incorporate advanced AI-powered technologies, including real-time ray tracing, revolutionizing game visuals with remarkable detail and realism.

**Processors** have also seen significant advancements, with AMD and Intel releasing multi-core CPUs capable of handling the escalating demands of modern games. The advent of PCIe 5.0, DDR5 memory, and innovative cooling technologies has facilitated faster data transfer speeds, enhanced overclocking capabilities, and overall superior performance.

Looking forward, virtual reality (VR) and augmented reality (AR) are gaining prominence, prompting gaming PCs to adapt to these immersive technologies. The rise of cloud gaming has further increased the versatility of gaming PCs, enabling gamers to play from virtually anywhere with an internet connection, even without high-end hardware. Additionally, the convergence of PC and console gaming experiences has blurred traditional boundaries, with devices like Valve's Steam Deck offering portable PC gaming with console-like convenience.

In summary, gaming PCs have evolved from basic systems capable of running simple games to sophisticated machines engineered for immersive, high-fidelity gaming experiences. As technology continues to advance, gaming PCs are poised to adapt and thrive, offering gamers unparalleled experiences in the years to come.

## Key Components and Their Roles

Building a high-performance gaming computer involves integrating several critical components, each playing a unique role in delivering an optimal gaming experience. Let's delve deeper into these components, exploring their functions, current technological advancements, and considerations for selecting the best options for your gaming needs.

### Central Processing Unit (CPU)

**The CPU,** often referred to as the brain of the computer, executes instructions required for programs to run, dictating tasks to all other components. In gaming, a powerful CPU is essential for handling complex calculations, including artificial intelligence (AI), physics simulations, and environmental interactions.

**As of 2025,** leading gaming CPUs are multi-core processors capable of managing multiple simultaneous processes. The AMD Ryzen 9 9950X3D and Intel's Core i9-13900K exemplify top-tier gaming processors, offering exceptional performance with their numerous cores and high clock speeds. These attributes facilitate efficient multitasking and higher frame rates in modern games.

**Graphics Processing Unit (GPU)**

The GPU is pivotal in rendering images, videos, and animations, transforming game data into visual output displayed on your monitor. High-end GPUs, such as Nvidia's RTX 50 series and AMD's Radeon RX 7000 series, enable gamers to enjoy smooth frame rates at high resolutions. They also support advanced features like ray tracing, which simulates realistic lighting effects, and Deep Learning Super Sampling (DLSS), an AI-driven technology that enhances image quality without compromising performance.

A robust GPU is crucial for modern gaming, particularly for playing at higher resolutions like 1440p or 4K, or with high refresh rates (144Hz or higher) to ensure ultra-smooth gameplay. For instance, the iBuyPower Y40 pre-built gaming PC, equipped with an RTX 4070 GPU, offers efficient performance at 1080p and 1440p resolutions, providing a cost-effective option for gamers seeking high-quality graphics.

**Memory (RAM)**

Random Access Memory (RAM) temporarily stores data actively processed by the CPU and GPU. Sufficient RAM allows the system to handle multiple tasks simultaneously without slowing down. Modern games are increasingly memory-intensive, with many requiring 16GB or more of RAM to run smoothly at higher settings. DDR4 and DDR5 RAM modules are common in contemporary systems, with DDR5 offering faster speeds and greater bandwidth, leading to improved load times and ensuring background processes don't interfere with gameplay.

## Storage

Storage solutions impact how quickly your operating system, games, and other files load and operate. Solid-State Drives (SSDs) are significantly faster than traditional Hard Disk Drives (HDDs), providing quicker load times and a more responsive system overall. NVMe SSDs, which connect directly to the motherboard via the PCIe interface, offer even higher speeds, reducing game loading times to mere seconds. For 2025, it's advisable to use an SSD with at least 1TB capacity for your primary drive to store your operating system and frequently played games. Additional storage, such as a secondary HDD or SSD, can accommodate larger games or files.

## Motherboard

The motherboard serves as the backbone of the gaming PC, connecting all components and ensuring effective communication between them. It contains slots for the CPU, RAM, GPU, and storage devices. When selecting a motherboard, consider its chipset, socket compatibility, and expansion options to ensure it supports your chosen components and allows for future upgrades. The motherboard also provides various ports for USB devices, audio systems, and networking. Features like Wi-Fi 6 and Bluetooth support are becoming standard, ensuring seamless connectivity to the internet and peripherals.

## Power Supply Unit (PSU)

The PSU provides power to all components in your system, making its quality and capacity crucial for system stability and longevity. Power requirements vary depending on the components used, particularly the CPU and GPU. A high-quality PSU ensures a stable power supply and protects components from power surges or fluctuations. For gaming PCs, selecting a PSU that provides sufficient wattage for all components, with some headroom for overclocking or future upgrades, is important. Typically, aim for at least 650W for mid-range builds and 850W or more for high-end systems.

**Cooling System**

Gaming PCs generate substantial heat, especially when running demanding titles or overclocking components. An efficient cooling system is essential to maintain optimal performance and prevent overheating. Cooling solutions come in two main types: air cooling and liquid cooling. Air cooling relies on fans and heatsinks to dissipate heat from components, while liquid cooling uses a closed-loop system to circulate coolant, providing more efficient heat dissipation. Liquid cooling is often preferred for overclocked systems or those with high-performance components, as it maintains lower temperatures and reduces the risk of thermal throttling.

## Assessing Your Gaming Needs

Understanding your specific gaming requirements is crucial for selecting appropriate components. Factors such as the types of games you play, desired resolution and refresh rates, and budget constraints significantly influence your build decisions.

### Game Genres and Requirements

The genres of games you play impact the system specifications you'll need. First-person shooters (FPS) and real-time strategy (RTS) games often require higher frame rates and faster response times, necessitating a powerful CPU and GPU. Role-playing games (RPGs), on the other hand, may emphasize detailed graphics and immersive worlds, benefiting from higher RAM and storage capacities. Understanding the requirements of your favorite games helps determine the necessary power and memory for your system.

## Resolution and Refresh Rate

The visual quality and responsiveness of your gaming experience are significantly influenced by your system's resolution and refresh rate capabilities. Resolution refers to the number of pixels displayed on the screen, with higher resolutions like 1440p (2560x1440 pixels) and 4K (3840x2160 pixels) offering sharper and more detailed images compared to standard 1080p (1920x1080 pixels). Refresh rate, measured in Hertz (Hz), indicates how many times per second the display updates its image; common refresh rates include 60Hz, 120Hz, 144Hz, and even 240Hz. A higher refresh rate results in smoother motion and improved responsiveness, which is particularly beneficial in fast-paced and competitive gaming scenarios.

To fully leverage high resolutions and refresh rates, your gaming PC must be equipped with components capable of delivering the necessary performance. This includes a powerful GPU and CPU that can handle the increased workload associated with rendering more pixels and maintaining high frame rates. For instance, achieving smooth gameplay at 1440p with a 144Hz refresh rate requires a system that can consistently output 144 frames per second (FPS). If your system falls short of this performance, you may not fully benefit from a high-refresh-rate monitor.

**Budget Considerations**

Balancing performance aspirations with financial constraints is a crucial aspect of building or upgrading a gaming PC. High-end components, such as the latest GPUs and CPUs, often come with premium price tags. It's essential to assess your gaming preferences and determine which components will provide the most significant impact on your experience. For example, if you primarily play less demanding titles or are content with 1080p resolution at 60Hz, investing in top-tier hardware may not be necessary. Conversely, if you aim to play the latest AAA games at ultra settings on a 4K monitor with a 144Hz refresh rate, allocating more of your budget toward a high-performance GPU and CPU would be prudent. Additionally, consider future-proofing your system by selecting components that allow for upgrades, ensuring longevity and adaptability as gaming technology evolves.

## Additional Considerations

*Monitor Selection*: The choice of monitor plays a pivotal role in your gaming experience. Features such as adaptive sync technologies (e.g., AMD FreeSync, NVIDIA G-SYNC) help synchronize the monitor's refresh rate with the GPU's output, reducing screen tearing and stuttering. Additionally, response time, color accuracy, and panel type (IPS, TN, VA) are factors that influence visual quality and performance. For instance, a monitor like Samsung's Odyssey G6 offers a 1440p resolution with a 240Hz refresh rate, providing a balance between high resolution and smooth gameplay.

*Peripheral Compatibility*: Ensure that your peripherals, such as keyboards, mice, and controllers, are compatible with your system and meet your gaming needs. Features like programmable buttons, customizable RGB lighting, and ergonomic designs can enhance your gaming experience.

*Networking*: A stable and fast internet connection is vital for online gaming. Consider using wired Ethernet connections for reduced latency, or ensure your motherboard supports the latest Wi-Fi standards (e.g., Wi-Fi 6) for reliable wireless performance.

**Audio**: Quality audio can significantly enhance immersion. Investing in a good set of speakers or gaming headphones with surround sound capabilities can provide a more engaging gaming environment.

**Aesthetics and Ergonomics**: Personalizing your gaming setup with aesthetic choices like RGB lighting and ensuring ergonomic arrangements can contribute to both comfort and enjoyment during extended gaming sessions.

By carefully considering these factors alongside the core components of your gaming PC, you can build a system tailored to your preferences and requirements, ensuring an optimal gaming experience.

# Chapter 2: Planning Your Gaming Rig

Building a high-performance gaming PC isn't just about selecting the most powerful parts available. It's a delicate balance that requires careful planning, a clear understanding of your gaming preferences, and ensuring all components are compatible with each other.

A well-built gaming rig can provide an immersive gaming experience, whether you're playing fast-paced shooters, expansive open-world RPGs, or high-resolution strategy games.

This chapter will walk you through the process of crafting a gaming PC that fits your budget while delivering the performance you need.

# Setting a Budget: Finding the Perfect Balance Between Cost and Performance

One of the most crucial steps in assembling a gaming PC is determining a realistic budget. While it may be tempting to splurge on top-tier hardware, overspending on certain components while neglecting others can lead to imbalanced performance. A gaming PC is a long-term investment, and making informed choices will ensure you get the most out of your money.

## How Much Should You Spend?

The budget you allocate for your gaming PC will largely depend on the types of games you play, the performance level you desire, and whether you plan to upgrade in the future. Below is a breakdown of common budget ranges and what you can expect from each:

**Entry-Level Build ($500–$800)**: Ideal for newcomers to PC gaming or casual players, an entry-level build focuses on affordability while still providing a solid gaming experience. You'll be able to play most modern titles at 1080p resolution with medium settings, achieving frame rates between 30–60 FPS. Key components in this price range include an AMD Ryzen 3 or Intel Core i3 processor, an Nvidia GTX 1650 or AMD Radeon RX 550 GPU, and 8GB of RAM.

**Mid-Tier Build ($800–$1,500)**: A mid-range system is well-suited for gamers who want a balance between performance and affordability. These builds can comfortably run modern games at high settings with frame rates between 60–120 FPS, supporting 1080p and even 1440p resolutions. This tier typically includes an AMD Ryzen 5 or Intel Core i5 processor, an Nvidia RTX 3060 or AMD Radeon RX 6600 GPU, and 16GB of RAM for smooth gameplay.

**High-End Build ($1,500–$3,000+)**: Enthusiasts looking for the best possible performance should consider a high-end gaming PC. This setup is designed for ultra-fast frame rates, high-resolution gaming at 1440p or 4K, and premium features such as ray tracing and VR capabilities. Expect components such as an AMD Ryzen 7 or Intel Core i7/i9 processor, an Nvidia RTX 4080/4090 or AMD Radeon RX 7900 XT GPU, and a minimum of 32GB of RAM, coupled with NVMe SSD storage for rapid data access.

## Maximizing Performance While Staying Within Budget

With a clear budget in mind, the next step is to allocate your funds wisely. The two most important components for gaming performance are the CPU and GPU, as they directly impact frame rates, graphical fidelity, and overall gameplay experience.

### Key Performance Components

**Processor (CPU)**: Responsible for handling game logic, artificial intelligence, and background tasks, a fast processor ensures your system runs smoothly, especially in CPU-intensive games. Budget-conscious gamers may opt for an AMD Ryzen 5 or Intel Core i5, while high-end users will benefit from an AMD Ryzen 7 or Intel Core i7/i9.

**Graphics Card (GPU)**: The GPU plays the biggest role in rendering visuals, determining the quality and smoothness of your gameplay. Nvidia's RTX and AMD's Radeon RX series offer various options, with budget-friendly choices like the RTX 3060 and high-end powerhouses like the RTX 4090 for 4K gaming.

**Other Essential Components and Cost Considerations**

While the CPU and GPU are the foundation of any gaming PC, other components also contribute to a well-rounded system. Here's a breakdown of additional key parts:

**Memory (RAM)**: For modern gaming, 16GB of DDR4 or DDR5 RAM is the ideal starting point. Competitive and high-performance setups may benefit from 32GB or more, especially for multitasking and content creation.

**Storage**: A 500GB or 1TB NVMe SSD is essential for fast load times and overall system responsiveness. If you require additional space for a large game library, consider adding a secondary HDD for mass storage.

**Motherboard**: Choosing the right motherboard ensures compatibility with your CPU, RAM, and GPU. Features such as PCIe 4.0 support, Wi-Fi capabilities, and future expandability should be considered based on your needs.

### Striking the Right Balance

When assembling a gaming PC, it's vital to create a system where each component complements the others. Avoid overspending on one part while neglecting another, as this can create performance bottlenecks. For example, investing in a high-end GPU while pairing it with an underpowered CPU could limit your frame rates due to CPU bottlenecks.

## Researching and Ensuring Component Compatibility

Once you have determined your budget and gaming needs, selecting compatible components is crucial to building a functional system.

### CPU and Motherboard Compatibility

The CPU and motherboard must match in terms of socket type and chipset support. For example, Intel's 12th and 13th Gen CPUs require an LGA 1700 motherboard, while AMD's Ryzen 7000 series processors need an AM5-compatible board. Additionally, ensure the motherboard supports features such as overclocking and high-speed RAM.

### GPU and Case Size Considerations

Graphics cards come in various sizes, and some high-end models are particularly large. Before purchasing, check the GPU's dimensions to ensure it fits inside your case. Smaller cases may require compact or dual-fan GPU variants.

**Storage Solutions**

For fast game load times and overall system responsiveness, an NVMe SSD is recommended. A 1TB NVMe SSD is a great starting point, with an additional HDD for bulk storage if needed. Ensure your motherboard has sufficient M.2 slots for future expansions.

**Conclusion**

Building a gaming PC is a strategic process that requires balancing performance and budget while ensuring compatibility among components. By understanding the demands of different game genres, selecting the appropriate resolution and refresh rate, and investing in future-proof hardware, you can build a system that delivers exceptional performance and longevity. Careful research and planning will allow you to create a gaming rig that meets your needs, whether you're aiming for high FPS in competitive shooters or immersive 4K RPG experiences.

## Defining Your Gaming Goals and Preferences

Before finalizing your component choices, consider the types of games you enjoy and the experience you want to achieve. Are you a competitive esports player looking for high refresh rates and low latency, or do you prefer visually stunning open-world adventures at maximum settings? Your gaming preferences will help determine the right balance of power and budget for your build.

By taking a structured approach—setting a budget, prioritizing critical components, and making informed choices—you can build a gaming PC that delivers an exceptional experience without overspending. In the next chapter, we'll dive deeper into selecting individual components and ensuring they work together seamlessly for optimal performance.

# Game Genres and Performance Considerations

When building a gaming PC, it's essential to recognize that different game genres place varying demands on your hardware. By understanding these requirements, you can allocate your budget more effectively to ensure optimal performance for your favorite types of games. Below is a breakdown of how different genres affect hardware choices:

## First-Person Shooters (FPS)

Games like *Call of Duty*, *Counter-Strike*, and *Overwatch* demand smooth gameplay, high frame rates, and low latency. Competitive FPS players benefit from a powerful GPU capable of sustaining high FPS and a high-refresh-rate monitor (120Hz or higher) to reduce motion blur and improve response time. A mid-tier CPU, such as an AMD Ryzen 5 or Intel Core i5, is generally sufficient for these games, as they are more GPU-intensive.

## Real-Time Strategy (RTS) and Multiplayer Online Battle Arena (MOBA) Games

Titles such as *StarCraft II*, *Age of Empires IV*, and *League of Legends* rely heavily on CPU performance, particularly for managing AI, unit interactions, and large-scale battles. A multi-core processor like an AMD Ryzen 7 or Intel Core i7 is ideal for handling these calculations smoothly. Since these games are typically not as graphically demanding, a mid-range GPU like the Nvidia RTX 3060 or AMD Radeon RX 6600 XT will suffice.

## Role-Playing Games (RPGs)

RPGs, including *The Witcher 3*, *Elden Ring*, and *Cyberpunk 2077*, require significant GPU power to render detailed open-world environments, character models, and visual effects. A high-end GPU, such as the Nvidia RTX 4070 or AMD Radeon RX 7800 XT, ensures smooth gameplay at high resolutions. Additionally, at least 16GB of RAM is recommended to handle large game worlds and background processes.

## Simulation and Strategy Games

Games like *The Sims 4*, *Cities: Skylines*, and *Microsoft Flight Simulator* require a strong CPU to manage detailed simulations and AI interactions. A powerful multi-threaded processor, such as an AMD Ryzen 9 or Intel Core i9, ensures smooth performance, while a mid-to-high-range GPU handles the visual elements. 32GB of RAM is ideal for resource-intensive simulations.

## Choosing the Right Resolution and Refresh Rate

The display resolution and refresh rate you aim for significantly impact your hardware choices. Higher resolutions require more powerful GPUs, while high refresh rates benefit from strong CPU and GPU combinations to maintain consistent performance.

## 1080p Gaming

For smooth gaming at 1080p, a budget to mid-range GPU, such as the Nvidia GTX 1660 Super or AMD Radeon RX 6600, is sufficient. These graphics cards can handle most modern games at high settings with frame rates between 60–144 FPS.

## 1440p Gaming

For those who prefer sharper visuals and better detail, 1440p gaming requires a more powerful GPU, such as the Nvidia RTX 3070 or AMD Radeon RX 6700 XT. This setup allows for smooth gameplay at high to ultra settings, typically running at 60–120 FPS, depending on the game.

## 4K Gaming

Gaming at 4K resolution demands top-tier GPUs, such as the Nvidia RTX 4080 or RTX 4090. These GPUs deliver high-quality visuals and smooth performance at 60 FPS or higher, especially in visually intensive games. Additionally, a high-end CPU like the Intel Core i9 or AMD Ryzen 9 is recommended to prevent bottlenecks.

**Future-Proofing Your Gaming PC**

Technology evolves rapidly, and a well-planned gaming PC should last several years before requiring significant upgrades. Future-proofing involves selecting components that offer scalability and longevity.

- **Motherboard:** Choose a motherboard with PCIe 4.0 or PCIe 5.0 support to ensure compatibility with future GPUs and storage solutions.
- **RAM:** Opting for 32GB of RAM instead of 16GB can provide longevity as games and applications become more memory-intensive.
- **Power Supply:** A high-quality PSU with at least 750W and an 80+ Gold certification ensures stability and accommodates future upgrades.

# Chapter 3: Essential Components for a High-Performance Gaming PC

Building a gaming PC requires a thorough understanding of each component's role in delivering smooth and immersive gameplay. Every part, from the processor that executes commands to the graphics card that renders stunning visuals, plays a crucial role in overall system performance.

This chapter will guide you through the key components necessary for a high-end gaming setup, their significance, recommended specifications for 2025, and best practices for installation and compatibility.

# Central Processing Unit (CPU): The Heart of System Performance

## Why the CPU Matters in Gaming

Often called the "brain" of the computer, the Central Processing Unit (CPU) handles computations and processes that power both the operating system and applications. In gaming, the CPU is responsible for logic-based functions, including artificial intelligence (AI), physics simulations, and multitasking.

While the Graphics Processing Unit (GPU) dominates in rendering visuals, the CPU ensures that background processes and in-game mechanics run seamlessly.

The demand for high-performance CPUs has increased, especially in modern open-world and strategy games that require complex calculations for AI-driven interactions and physics-based environments. A powerful processor prevents bottlenecking, ensuring the GPU performs at its full potential.

**Top CPU Picks for 2025**

Both AMD and Intel continue to offer top-tier processors tailored for gaming. Here are the best options to consider:

- **AMD Ryzen 9 7950X**: A powerhouse with 16 cores and 32 threads, this CPU excels in both multi-threaded and single-threaded performance, making it ideal for demanding games and content creation.
- **Intel Core i9-13900K**: Featuring a hybrid architecture with performance and efficiency cores, this processor optimizes speed and power efficiency, making it a great choice for high-end gaming and multitasking.
- **AMD Ryzen 7 7800X3D**: Known for its impressive single-core speeds, this CPU offers a balance between performance and cost,

making it a strong choice for gamers prioritizing high frame rates.

- **Intel Core i7-13700K**: A cost-effective alternative to the i9 series, this CPU delivers excellent gaming performance with its combination of performance and efficiency cores.

## Installation and Compatibility Considerations

Before purchasing a CPU, ensure it's compatible with your motherboard's socket type and chipset. For example, the AMD Ryzen 9 7950X requires an **AM5** socket motherboard, while Intel's Core i9-13900K fits the **LGA 1700** socket.

During installation, align the CPU properly within the socket, apply thermal paste for efficient heat transfer, and secure the cooling solution. Handle the processor carefully to avoid damaging the delicate pins or contacts.

# Graphics Processing Unit (GPU): The Key to Stunning Visuals

## Why the GPU Is Crucial for Gaming

The Graphics Processing Unit (GPU) is responsible for rendering images, textures, lighting, and visual effects in video games. A powerful GPU ensures high frame rates, detailed textures, and smooth gameplay, particularly in graphically demanding titles.

## Top GPUs for 2025

The latest GPU models from Nvidia and AMD push gaming visuals to new heights:

- **Nvidia GeForce RTX 4090**: The ultimate GPU for 4K gaming, featuring **24GB of GDDR6X memory** and advanced technologies like **DLSS 3.0** and real-time ray tracing.
- **AMD Radeon RX 7900 XTX**: A high-performance alternative that rivals the RTX

4090, offering excellent 1440p and 4K gaming capabilities at a competitive price.

- **Nvidia GeForce RTX 4070 Ti**: An ideal mid-range choice for gamers seeking a balance between price and performance, supporting **ray tracing** and high refresh rates at 1440p resolution.
- **AMD Radeon RX 7800 XT**: A cost-effective option for gamers targeting high frame rates at 1440p without sacrificing graphical fidelity.

**Installation and Optimization Tips**

To install a GPU, insert it into the **PCIe x16 slot** on the motherboard, secure it with screws, and connect the necessary **PCIe power cables** from the power supply. Ensure the case has adequate space and ventilation to prevent overheating. Regularly updating GPU drivers is essential for maintaining optimal performance and compatibility with the latest games.

# Motherboard: The Foundation of Your Gaming Rig

## Choosing the Right Motherboard

The motherboard acts as the backbone of your PC, linking all components together. It determines the system's expansion capabilities, including RAM slots, PCIe lanes, and storage options. When selecting a motherboard, ensure it supports your CPU, GPU, and memory requirements.

## Key Factors to Consider

- **Socket Type**: Ensure compatibility with your chosen CPU (e.g., AM5 for Ryzen 7000 series, LGA 1700 for Intel 13th Gen).
- **Chipset**: High-end chipsets like **AMD X670** and **Intel Z690** offer better overclocking support and additional features.
- **Form Factor**: **ATX motherboards** provide more expansion slots, while **microATX** and

**mini-ITX** options are suited for compact builds.

## Installation Best Practices

Mount the motherboard securely inside the case, ensuring proper alignment with standoff screws. Connect the **24-pin power cable**, **CPU power connectors**, and essential headers for seamless operation.

# Memory (RAM): Speed and Efficiency for Gaming

## Why RAM Matters

RAM stores temporary data that the CPU and GPU frequently access. Faster and higher-capacity RAM ensures smoother gameplay, particularly in open-world and multiplayer games.

## Recommended RAM Specifications

- **16GB DDR5** (5200MHz or higher) is the ideal baseline for gaming in 2025.
- **32GB DDR5** is recommended for high-end setups, especially for streaming or content creation.

**Installation and Configuration**

Install RAM modules in the correct slots to enable **dual-channel** or **quad-channel** configurations for improved bandwidth. Verify speeds in the **BIOS settings** to ensure they run at the advertised frequency.

## Storage: Faster Load Times for Seamless Gaming

**SSD vs. HDD: Which One to Choose?**

- **NVMe SSDs** offer lightning-fast load times and are recommended for gaming.
- **SATA SSDs** provide a more affordable but slightly slower alternative.

- **HDDs** are best suited for mass storage of media files and backup purposes.

## Recommended Storage Setup

A **1TB NVMe SSD** is ideal for fast game loading, while a secondary **2TB HDD** provides additional storage for game libraries and media.

# Power Supply Unit (PSU): Reliable Power for Stability

## Choosing the Right PSU

A high-quality PSU ensures stable power delivery and prevents system failures. Calculate power requirements based on your components and opt for an **80+ Gold** or **Platinum-certified PSU**.

## Recommended Wattage

- **750W-850W** for mid-range builds
- **1000W+** for high-end setups with power-hungry GPUs

**Installation Tips**

Secure the PSU in the case, connect **24-pin and 8-pin CPU power cables**, and ensure proper cable management to maintain airflow and aesthetics.

## Cooling Systems

**Air vs. Liquid Cooling**

Effective cooling is crucial for maintaining optimal performance in a gaming PC. Air cooling uses fans and heatsinks to dissipate heat, while liquid cooling uses a closed-loop system to circulate coolant and keep temperatures low. Liquid cooling is more efficient and quieter but is typically more expensive and complex to install.

**Choosing the Right Cooling Solution**

For most gaming PCs, high-quality air-cooling solutions are sufficient. However, if you plan to overclock your CPU or GPU, or if you're building a high-performance system, liquid cooling might be a better option. Ensure that your case has enough space for the cooling solution you choose and that your motherboard supports the required mounting points.

## Installation and Maintenance

Installing air cooling involves mounting the heatsink and fan onto the CPU and securing them in place. Liquid cooling requires more setup, including mounting the radiator and connecting the pump and tubing. Regular maintenance, including cleaning dust filters and ensuring fans are functioning properly, will ensure your cooling system performs optimally.

Conclusion

Building a high-performance gaming PC requires careful selection of each component to ensure they work together seamlessly. From the CPU and GPU to RAM, storage, and cooling solutions, each part plays a vital role in delivering the best possible gaming experience. By choosing the right components and following installation best practices, you'll create a system capable of handling the most demanding games in 2025 and beyond.

# Chapter 4: Building Your Gaming PC

Building your own gaming PC is an exciting and rewarding journey, offering the freedom to customize every component to suit your gaming needs. Not only does it provide a deeper understanding of your system's inner workings, but it also ensures optimal performance tailored to your preferences.

In this chapter, we will walk you through the entire process of assembling your gaming PC, from preparing your workspace to setting up the BIOS and installing your operating system. By following this guide, you will gain confidence in constructing a high-performance rig that delivers an immersive gaming experience.

# Preparing Your Workspace

Before diving into the assembly process, setting up a proper workspace is essential to ensure efficiency and safety. A well-organized environment minimizes the risk of component damage and reduces stress during the build. Here's how to prepare your space effectively:

## 1. Choose a Clean and Spacious Area

Find a stable, flat surface like a sturdy table or desk with ample room to lay out all your components. Avoid working in a cluttered or cramped space, as this can lead to misplaced screws or accidental damage to fragile parts.

## 2. Gather Essential Tools

Having the right tools at your disposal will streamline the build process. The fundamental tools you will need include:

- **Phillips-head screwdriver** (preferably magnetic to hold small screws securely)
- **Anti-static wrist strap** (to prevent electrostatic discharge that could harm sensitive components)
- **Thermal paste applicator** (if your CPU cooler does not come with pre-applied thermal paste)
- **Tweezers or small pliers** (for handling tiny screws and connectors)
- **Cable ties or Velcro straps** (for efficient cable management)

## 3. Take Static Precautions

Electrostatic discharge (ESD) can damage delicate PC components. To prevent this:

- Wear an **anti-static wrist strap** and attach it to a grounded metal object.

- Avoid working on carpeted floors or wearing woolen clothing, as they generate static electricity.
- Frequently touch an unpainted metal part of your PC case to discharge any built-up static.

## 4. Organize and Inspect Components

Unpack all your PC parts and organize them neatly in your workspace. Check each component for any visible damage before starting the build. This will save time and prevent complications later in the assembly process.

## Step-by-Step Assembly Guide

With your workspace prepared, let's begin assembling your gaming PC. Follow these steps carefully to ensure a smooth and efficient build.

## Installing the CPU and Cooler

## 1. Prepare the CPU Socket

Locate the CPU socket on your motherboard. Lift the retention arm or socket cover, ensuring you do not touch the delicate pins inside the socket.

## 2. Install the CPU

- Hold the processor by its edges to avoid contact with the pins or gold contacts.
- Align the CPU with the socket using the notches or arrows as guides.
- Gently place the CPU into the socket without applying force.
- Lower the retention arm to secure the CPU in place.

## 3. Apply Thermal Paste

If your CPU cooler does not come with pre-applied thermal paste, apply a **pea-sized dot** in the center of the CPU. Avoid using too much, as excessive paste can hinder heat dissipation.

## 4. Install the CPU Cooler

- Position the cooler over the CPU, aligning it with the mounting holes.
- Secure it in place using screws or clips, depending on the cooler type.
- Connect the cooler's power cable to the CPU fan header on the motherboard.

## Mounting the Motherboard

### 1. Prepare the Case

- Remove the side panels of your PC case to allow easy access.
- Install the motherboard's **I/O shield** (the metal plate that covers the rear ports) into the case.
- Screw in the motherboard standoffs to prevent direct contact with the metal case, reducing the risk of short circuits.

### 2. Position and Secure the Motherboard

- Align the motherboard with the I/O shield and standoffs.
- Carefully lower it into place, ensuring the ports fit correctly through the I/O shield.
- Secure the motherboard with screws, tightening them evenly.

## Installing RAM and Storage Drives

### 1. Install RAM Modules

- Locate the **DIMM slots** on the motherboard.
- Insert RAM sticks into the correct slots (refer to the motherboard manual for dual-channel configuration).
- Press down firmly until the locking clips snap into place.

### 2. Install Storage Devices

- For an **M.2 NVMe SSD**, insert it at an angle into the M.2 slot and secure it with a small screw.

- For **SATA SSDs or HDDs**, mount them in the drive bays, secure them with screws, and connect power and data cables.

## Installing the GPU

### 1. Prepare the PCIe Slot

Remove the metal expansion slot covers at the back of the case where the GPU will be installed.

### 2. Insert and Secure the GPU

- Align the graphics card with the **PCIe x16 slot** and press it down firmly until it clicks.
- Secure it with screws to prevent movement.
- Connect the appropriate **PCIe power cables** from the PSU to the GPU.

## Connecting the PSU and Cable Management

### 1. Install the PSU

- Place the PSU in its designated compartment, ensuring proper ventilation.

- Secure it with screws to keep it stable.

## 2. Connect Power Cables

- **24-pin cable** to the motherboard
- **8-pin CPU power connector** to the CPU power slot
- **PCIe power cables** to the GPU
- **SATA power connectors** to storage drives

## 3. Manage Cables for Airflow

Use cable ties to organize wires neatly, keeping them away from cooling fans and airflow paths.

## First Boot and BIOS Configuration

Once assembly is complete, it's time to power on the system and configure the BIOS.

## 1. Power On the System

- Double-check all connections before pressing the power button.

- If the PC does not start, troubleshoot by ensuring cables are correctly connected and components are seated properly.

## 2. Enter BIOS Setup

- Upon booting, press the **BIOS access key** (typically Del or F2).
- Check that all components are correctly detected.
- Enable **XMP (Extreme Memory Profile)** to optimize RAM performance.
- Set the **boot order** to prioritize your storage device with the OS installer.

## 3. Update BIOS

- Check for the latest firmware updates from the motherboard manufacturer's website and apply them if necessary.

# Installing the Operating System

Once your gaming PC has been successfully assembled and powered on, the next crucial step is installing the operating system (OS). This process ensures that your system can function properly and take full advantage of its hardware capabilities.

## 1. Create a Bootable USB Drive

Before installing the OS, you need a bootable USB drive that contains the operating system installation files. Follow these steps:

- **Download the OS:** Visit the official website of your preferred operating system, such as Windows 11 or a Linux distribution (e.g., Ubuntu, Fedora, or Arch Linux).
- **Prepare a USB Flash Drive:** Use a USB drive with at least 8GB of storage for Windows or 4GB for Linux.
- **Use a Bootable USB Creation Tool:** Download and install a tool such as:

- Rufus (for Windows and Linux installations)
- Windows Media Creation Tool (for Windows 10/11)
- BalenaEtcher (for Linux and macOS)
- Create the Bootable Drive: Open the tool, select the OS installation file (ISO), choose your USB drive, and follow the on-screen instructions to create a bootable USB installer.

## 2. Install the Operating System

Now that you have a bootable USB drive ready, it's time to install the OS:

1. **Insert the USB Drive:** Plug the bootable USB into a USB port on your PC.
2. **Restart and Enter BIOS:** Restart your system and immediately press the BIOS key (usually F2, F12, Delete, or Esc, depending on your motherboard) to access the BIOS settings.

3. **Select the Boot Device:** In the BIOS menu, navigate to the Boot Order section and set the USB drive as the primary boot device.

4. **Start Installation:** Save changes and exit the BIOS. Your PC will restart and load the OS installer from the USB drive.

5. Follow On-Screen Prompts:

    o Choose your preferred language, region, and keyboard layout.

    o Select Custom Installation (for a fresh install).

    o Choose your primary storage device (SSD for optimal performance).

    o If needed, partition the drive to allocate space for different storage needs.

6. **Begin the Installation:** Click Install and let the OS installation process complete. This may take 5 to 30 minutes, depending on your hardware speed.

## 3. Complete System Setup

Once the OS is installed, follow these steps to finalize your setup:

- **Create a User Account:** Enter your name and set up a password for security.
- **Configure Privacy Settings:** Choose your privacy preferences, such as data sharing options and location services.
- **Connect to the Internet:** Use Wi-Fi or an Ethernet cable to establish an internet connection.
- **Update the OS:** Install the latest security updates and system patches for performance improvements.

## 4. Install Necessary Drivers

To ensure smooth performance, install the required drivers for your hardware components:

- Motherboard Drivers: Download chipset, audio, LAN, and USB drivers from the motherboard manufacturer's website.

- Graphics Card Drivers: Visit the official NVIDIA (GeForce Experience) or AMD (Radeon Software) website to download and install the latest GPU drivers.
- Peripheral Drivers: Install additional drivers for your gaming mouse, keyboard, headset, and controllers if needed.

## 5. Optimize and Customize Your System

After installing the drivers, optimize your PC for gaming:

- **Adjust Display Settings:** Set your monitor's refresh rate (e.g., 144Hz, 240Hz) and resolution in the display settings.
- **Enable XMP for RAM:** Go to the BIOS and enable XMP (Extreme Memory Profile) to ensure your RAM runs at its rated speed.
- **Download Essential Apps:** Install a web browser, gaming platforms (Steam, Epic Games, Xbox Game Pass, etc.), and system

monitoring tools like HWMonitor or MSI Afterburner.

Conclusion

Building a gaming PC is an exciting and rewarding experience that allows you to customize every aspect of your machine for maximum performance and efficiency. By carefully assembling each component, setting up the BIOS, and installing the operating system, you've successfully created a powerful, high-performance gaming rig.

Now that your system is up and running, it's time to:

- Install your favorite games and test your hardware's capabilities.
- Fine-tune your settings for smooth gameplay and optimal FPS.
- Keep your system updated to ensure peak performance and security.

With your custom-built PC, you can now enjoy a next-level gaming experience—whether you're battling in competitive esports, immersing yourself in story-driven adventures, or pushing the limits of 4K and high-refresh-rate gaming.

Your journey into PC gaming has just begun—welcome to the world of limitless possibilities!

# Chapter 5: Optimizing Your Gaming Rig

Once your gaming PC is fully assembled and running, the next crucial step is optimization. While having powerful hardware is essential, ensuring that your system is fine-tuned for maximum efficiency can make a significant difference in gaming performance. A well-optimized gaming rig can deliver smoother frame rates, reduced lag, and better system stability, enhancing your overall gaming experience.

This chapter covers essential techniques for optimizing your system, including updating drivers and firmware, safely overclocking your components, configuring in-game settings for peak performance, and utilizing performance monitoring tools. By following these steps, you can ensure that your gaming PC runs at its best, providing an immersive and uninterrupted gaming experience.

# Updating Drivers and Firmware

Keeping your system up to date is one of the most important steps in optimizing your gaming rig. Drivers allow your operating system to communicate with your hardware, while firmware controls the low-level functionality of your components. Regular updates can enhance performance, fix bugs, and improve security.

## Why Updating Drivers and Firmware Is Important

- **Performance Enhancements**: GPU and chipset manufacturers frequently release driver updates that optimize performance for new games, improve stability, and sometimes even boost frame rates.
- **Bug Fixes**: Updated drivers can resolve issues such as crashes, screen tearing, and stuttering that might be affecting your gaming experience.

- **Security Patches**: Keeping firmware up to date helps protect your system from vulnerabilities that could be exploited by malware or hackers.

**How to Update Drivers**

1. **Graphics Card Drivers**: The most critical driver for gaming is your GPU driver. Depending on whether you have an NVIDIA or AMD graphics card, follow these steps:

   - **NVIDIA**: Use the GeForce Experience app to check for updates and install the latest drivers automatically.
   - **AMD**: Use the Radeon Software Adrenalin Edition to update drivers and optimize performance settings.
   - **Manual Updates**: You can also download the latest drivers directly from the NVIDIA or AMD website and install them manually.

2. **Motherboard and Chipset Drivers**: These drivers ensure proper communication between your CPU, RAM, and storage devices.

   o Visit the motherboard manufacturer's website (ASUS, MSI, Gigabyte, ASRock, etc.) and download the latest chipset and BIOS/UEFI updates.

   o Install drivers for onboard network adapters, audio controllers, and storage controllers.

3. **Peripheral Drivers**: Keyboards, mice, gaming headsets, and controllers often have software that enhances functionality and customization.

   o Update drivers via the manufacturer's website or dedicated software like Logitech G HUB or Razer Synapse.

**How to Update Firmware**

1. **BIOS/UEFI Updates**:

- Check your motherboard manufacturer's support page for BIOS updates.
- Most modern motherboards have an easy-to-use BIOS update utility (e.g., ASUS EZ Flash or MSI M-Flash).
- Follow the manufacturer's instructions carefully to avoid bricking your motherboard.

2. **SSD and Storage Firmware**:
   - Check for firmware updates from SSD manufacturers such as Samsung, Crucial, or Western Digital.
   - Use utilities like Samsung Magician to update SSD firmware and enable performance-enhancing features like TRIM.

## Overclocking for Enhanced Performance

Overclocking allows your CPU, GPU, and RAM to run at higher speeds than their factory defaults, leading to improved gaming performance. However, improper overclocking can cause instability, excessive heat, and potential hardware damage.

**Safe Overclocking Practices**

1. **Start with Small Increments**
   - Increase CPU clock speed in small steps (e.g., 100 MHz at a time) and test stability after each change.
   - GPU overclocking can be done using MSI Afterburner or EVGA Precision X1, adjusting core and memory clocks incrementally.

2. **Monitor Temperatures**
   - Overclocking generates extra heat, so use monitoring software like HWMonitor or CoreTemp to ensure CPU/GPU temperatures remain within safe limits.
   - Invest in high-performance cooling solutions such as an aftermarket air cooler or liquid cooling system.

3. **Adjust Voltage Cautiously**
   - Increasing voltage (Vcore) may be necessary for stability but also raises heat output.
   - Avoid excessive overvolting to prevent long-term damage to components.
4. **Stress Test Your System**
   - Use Prime95 for CPU stress testing and FurMark for GPU stress testing.
   - Run stability tests for at least 30 minutes to ensure the overclock is reliable.

# Configuring Game Settings for Optimal Performance

Even with a powerful gaming rig, configuring your in-game settings correctly can make a substantial difference in performance.

**Key Settings to Adjust**

1. **Resolution and Refresh Rate**

- Ensure your monitor's refresh rate is correctly set (e.g., 144Hz for a 144Hz monitor).
- Lowering the resolution (e.g., from 4K to 1440p) can significantly boost frame rates if needed.

2. **Graphics Quality**
   - Reduce settings like shadows, ambient occlusion, and anti-aliasing to improve FPS without heavily impacting visual quality.

3. **V-Sync and Frame Limiting**
   - Enabling V-Sync prevents screen tearing but may introduce input lag.
   - G-Sync (NVIDIA) and FreeSync (AMD) offer smoother gameplay without the downsides of traditional V-Sync.

4. **Use DirectX or Vulkan API**
   - Some games offer multiple rendering APIs (e.g., DirectX 12 or Vulkan). Experiment with different APIs to find

the best balance of performance and visual quality for your system.

5. **Field of View (FOV) Adjustments**

   o A wider FOV increases GPU load. Lowering FOV slightly can improve FPS in demanding games.

## Utilizing Performance Monitoring Tools

Monitoring your system's performance can help you detect bottlenecks, overheating, or underperforming hardware.

**Recommended Performance Monitoring Tools**

1. **MSI Afterburner**: Displays real-time stats like GPU temperature, clock speeds, and frame rates.
2. **HWMonitor**: Tracks CPU/GPU temps, fan speeds, and power consumption.

3. **CPU-Z & GPU-Z**: Provides detailed information on your CPU and GPU specifications and performance metrics.

4. **FPS Counters**: Use Fraps or Rivatuner Statistics Server (RTSS) to display FPS while gaming.

5. **Benchmarking Tools**:
   - **3DMark**: GPU benchmarking tool for measuring performance.
   - **Cinebench**: CPU performance benchmarking.
   - **Unigine Heaven**: Tests GPU stability and performance.

Conclusion

Optimizing your gaming rig involves a combination of updating software, fine-tuning hardware settings, and configuring games for smooth performance. By keeping drivers and firmware updated, overclocking safely, adjusting game settings intelligently, and monitoring your system's performance, you can significantly enhance your gaming experience. With the right optimizations, your gaming PC will be more stable, efficient, and capable of handling the latest games with ease.

# Chapter 6: Advanced Enhancements

After fine-tuning your gaming PC's foundational components, it's time to take things a step further by implementing advanced enhancements. These upgrades not only improve performance and efficiency but also allow for a more personalized and immersive gaming experience.

From modifying your PC case for aesthetic and functional improvements to enhancing cooling solutions, setting up multi-GPU configurations, and harnessing cutting-edge technologies such as Virtual Reality (VR) and ray tracing, there are numerous ways to optimize your system.

This chapter delves into these advanced enhancements, helping you unleash the full potential of your gaming rig.

# Customizing Your PC Case for Aesthetics and Functionality

A gaming PC case does more than just house essential components; it plays a vital role in airflow, cooling, and overall system efficiency. Additionally, customization options allow you to showcase your style and create a setup that stands out.

## Selecting the Ideal PC Case

The foundation of a well-optimized gaming rig begins with choosing the right PC case. The ideal choice depends on your personal preference, available space, and the hardware you plan to install. Here are the most common types of PC cases:

- **Mid-Tower Cases**: The most popular option, offering a balance between size and expandability. These cases accommodate standard ATX motherboards and provide enough room for most gaming builds.

- **Full-Tower Cases**: Designed for enthusiasts requiring extra space for multiple GPUs, custom cooling solutions, and extensive storage options. Ideal for high-performance builds.
- **Small Form Factor (SFF) Cases**: Compact and space-saving, perfect for minimalistic setups. However, they require careful planning for cooling and hardware compatibility.

When selecting a case, ensure it supports your motherboard form factor (ATX, microATX, or Mini-ITX), GPU size, and desired cooling system. Many modern cases feature tempered glass side panels, tool-less design, and RGB integration, adding both style and convenience.

## Aesthetic and Personalization Enhancements

Once you've chosen your case, there are various ways to customize its appearance:

- **RGB Lighting**: RGB lighting has become a standard feature in gaming PCs, offering dynamic color customization. Components like RAM sticks, fans, CPU coolers, and LED strips can be synchronized using software like Corsair iCUE, Razer Chroma, or ASUS Aura Sync.

- **Cable Management**: Organized cables not only improve aesthetics but also optimize airflow. Use Velcro straps, cable routing channels, and PSU shrouds to maintain a clean and clutter-free setup.

- **Custom Side Panels**: Some gamers opt for personalized panels featuring engraved designs, logos, or artwork inspired by their favorite games.

- **Liquid Cooling Displays**: High-end builds often integrate custom water loops with colored coolant, transparent tubing, and reservoir displays to create visually stunning rigs.

# Implementing Advanced Cooling Solutions for Optimal Performance

As gaming hardware becomes more powerful, managing heat dissipation is crucial for stability and longevity. Implementing efficient cooling methods prevents thermal throttling and ensures your components run at peak performance.

## Air Cooling Optimization

Traditional air cooling remains a reliable and cost-effective method for most gaming setups. To maximize airflow and heat dissipation:

- **Strategic Fan Placement**: A well-balanced airflow setup includes front intake fans drawing in cool air and top/rear exhaust fans expelling hot air.
- **High-Performance CPU Coolers**: Upgrading to a tower-style air cooler from brands like Noctua or be quiet! provides enhanced cooling compared to stock coolers.

- **Positive vs. Negative Pressure**: Positive pressure (more intake fans) helps reduce dust accumulation, while negative pressure (more exhaust fans) enhances cooling efficiency.

## Liquid Cooling Solutions

For those pushing their hardware to the limits, liquid cooling is an advanced alternative:

- **All-in-One (AIO) Coolers**: Pre-assembled water cooling units provide efficient cooling with minimal maintenance. Popular models include Corsair iCUE H150i and NZXT Kraken X-series.
- **Custom Water Cooling Loops**: Enthusiasts seeking maximum cooling efficiency can design custom loops with reservoirs, radiators, and liquid coolant. This setup requires careful planning but offers superior thermal performance.

Regular maintenance, such as cleaning radiators and changing coolant, is necessary to maintain optimal cooling efficiency over time.

## Setting Up Multi-GPU Configurations: Are They Still Worth It?

For years, multi-GPU setups were a go-to solution for high-end gaming and professional workloads. However, recent advancements in single-GPU performance and declining software support have changed the landscape.

### Understanding SLI and CrossFire

Nvidia's **SLI (Scalable Link Interface)** and AMD's **CrossFire** once allowed gamers to run multiple GPUs in parallel. However, many modern titles no longer support multi-GPU scaling, leading to diminishing returns. Additionally, issues such as micro-stuttering, driver incompatibility, and high power consumption make multi-GPU setups less viable for gaming today.

## Key Considerations for Multi-GPU Builds

If you still wish to explore a multi-GPU setup, ensure the following:

1. **Motherboard Compatibility**: Choose a motherboard with multiple PCIe x16 slots and adequate bandwidth.
2. **Power Supply Requirements**: Multi-GPU setups demand high-wattage power supplies (typically 850W+).
3. **Driver Support**: Ensure that your games and applications fully utilize multi-GPU configurations.

For most gamers, investing in a powerful single GPU like the **RTX 4090** or **RX 7900 XTX** provides better results than a dual-GPU setup.

# Virtual Reality (VR) and Ray Tracing Technologies: The Future of Gaming

Emerging technologies like VR and ray tracing are reshaping the gaming industry, providing unparalleled levels of realism and immersion.

**Virtual Reality (VR) Gaming**

VR gaming delivers an interactive experience by placing players inside the virtual world using a headset. Some of the leading VR headsets include:

- **Meta Quest 2**: Standalone or PC-tethered VR headset offering great value.
- **Valve Index**: Premium VR headset with superior tracking and refresh rates.
- **PlayStation VR2**: Designed for seamless integration with PlayStation consoles.

**Setting Up VR on Your PC**

1. **Hardware Requirements**: VR gaming demands a high-performance GPU (RTX

3070+ or RX 6800 XT), at least 16GB of RAM, and a strong CPU.

2. **Software Installation**: Platforms like SteamVR or Oculus Software are essential for running VR applications.

3. **Play Area Configuration**: A minimum space of 6.5ft x 6.5ft is recommended for room-scale VR gaming.

Popular VR titles such as *Half-Life: Alyx* and *Beat Saber* showcase the potential of immersive gaming experiences.

**Ray Tracing: Next-Level Visual Fidelity**

Ray tracing is a real-time rendering technique that simulates realistic lighting, shadows, and reflections. Nvidia's **RTX series** and AMD's **RDNA 2/3 GPUs** support ray tracing, enhancing graphical quality in supported games.

**Enabling Ray Tracing in Games**

1. **Game Settings**: Enable ray tracing from the graphics menu in supported titles.

2. **DLSS and FSR**: Nvidia's **DLSS (Deep Learning Super Sampling)** and AMD's **FSR (FidelityFX Super Resolution)** help maintain smooth frame rates while using ray tracing.

3. **Performance Impact**: While ray tracing significantly improves visuals, it can reduce frame rates. Adjust settings for an optimal balance between performance and image quality.

Notable ray-traced games include *Cyberpunk 2077*, *Control*, and *Minecraft RTX*.

## Conclusion

Advanced gaming PC enhancements offer countless ways to improve performance, aesthetics, and immersion. Whether you're customizing your case, optimizing cooling solutions, experimenting with multi-GPU setups, or embracing VR and ray tracing, these upgrades elevate your gaming experience to new heights. Investing in the latest hardware and optimizing configurations ensures your system remains future-proof, delivering the best possible gaming experience for years to come.

# Chapter 7: Troubleshooting and Maintenance

Building or owning a gaming PC is a rewarding experience, but maintaining its performance over time requires attention and care. Regardless of how well-assembled or optimized your system is, occasional technical issues will arise. These problems can range from minor inconveniences like system lag to severe complications such as hardware failure.

Understanding how to diagnose common issues, conduct routine maintenance, and upgrade components effectively will not only enhance the longevity of your system but also ensure that it remains powerful enough to handle evolving gaming demands. Additionally, as gaming technology advances, upgrading certain components will be necessary to keep your system relevant and capable of running the latest titles at peak performance.

In this chapter, we will delve into troubleshooting the most frequent gaming PC issues, provide essential maintenance tips, and explore how to future-proof your build through strategic upgrades.

## Diagnosing Common Gaming PC Issues

No matter how carefully a gaming rig is built, performance problems can surface over time. Recognizing the symptoms of common issues and knowing how to address them can save you time and prevent unnecessary stress. Below, we break down some of the most frequent problems gamers encounter and the steps to troubleshoot them.

### 1. Power or Boot Failure

If your PC refuses to turn on or fails to boot into the operating system, several factors could be at play. Here's how to diagnose and resolve the issue:

- **Check Power Supply Connections:** Ensure all power cables from the power supply unit (PSU) are properly connected to the motherboard, GPU, and storage drives. Sometimes, a loose connection can prevent the system from powering on.

- **Test the PSU:** If the system is unresponsive, the PSU could be defective. You can test it using the paperclip method or a PSU tester to verify power output. If the PSU is malfunctioning, replace it with a model that provides adequate wattage for your components.

- **Inspect the Motherboard and CPU:** Look for physical signs of damage on the motherboard, such as burned areas or swollen capacitors. Also, ensure that the CPU is seated correctly in its socket and that the cooler is firmly attached.

- **Disconnect Peripherals:** External devices like USB drives, additional monitors, or faulty peripherals may interfere with booting.

Disconnect all non-essential peripherals and attempt to start the system again.

## 2. Overheating and Thermal Throttling

Overheating is a common concern, particularly when running demanding games or overclocking components. Prolonged exposure to high temperatures can lead to performance drops, crashes, or even permanent hardware damage.

Here's how to mitigate overheating issues:

- **Ensure Proper Airflow:** Good airflow is crucial for keeping components cool. Arrange case fans in a balanced intake-exhaust configuration to promote air circulation.
- **Clean Fans and Heatsinks:** Dust accumulation can block ventilation, reducing cooling efficiency. Regularly clean fans, heatsinks, and air filters using compressed air.
- **Monitor Temperatures:** Utilize software like HWMonitor, MSI Afterburner, or

CoreTemp to track CPU and GPU temperatures. Ideally, CPU temperatures should stay below 75°C, and GPUs should remain under 85°C during gaming sessions.

- **Reapply Thermal Paste:** Over time, thermal paste can dry out, diminishing heat transfer between the CPU/GPU and their coolers. Reapplying high-quality thermal paste every 1-2 years can help maintain optimal temperatures.

- **Consider Aftermarket Cooling:** If overheating persists, upgrading to a more powerful air cooler or an all-in-one (AIO) liquid cooling system can significantly reduce temperatures.

## 3. Lag, Stuttering, and Slow Performance

Even high-end gaming PCs can experience performance drops. Here's how to diagnose and resolve slow performance:

- **Update Drivers:** Keeping your GPU drivers up to date ensures that your hardware runs optimally. Use NVIDIA GeForce Experience or AMD Radeon Software to install the latest updates.

- **Disable Background Applications:** Open Task Manager and close unnecessary applications consuming CPU, RAM, or disk resources while gaming.

- **Adjust In-Game Settings:** High graphical settings, such as ultra textures or excessive post-processing effects, can tax your GPU. Reducing settings like anti-aliasing and shadows can improve frame rates.

- **Upgrade RAM and Storage:** If your PC has less than 16GB of RAM or your storage drive is nearing capacity, upgrading to additional RAM or a faster SSD can improve overall system responsiveness.

## 4. Random Crashes and Freezes

Game crashes or system freezes can be due to hardware instability, corrupted files, or software conflicts. Troubleshoot as follows:

- **Check for Overheating:** Use monitoring tools to ensure your CPU and GPU aren't overheating during gameplay.
- **Test RAM for Errors:** Faulty RAM can cause crashes. Use MemTest86 to check for memory corruption.
- **Scan for Corrupt Files:** Run Windows System File Checker (sfc /scannow) to identify and repair corrupted system files.
- **Stress Test Components:** Use stress-testing software like Prime95 for CPU testing and FurMark for GPU stability. If crashes occur, the affected component may need replacement or reconfiguration.

# Routine Maintenance for Optimal Performance

Regular upkeep is essential for keeping your gaming PC running efficiently. Follow these maintenance practices:

1. **Regular Cleaning:**
   - Use compressed air to remove dust from fans, vents, and heatsinks.
   - Clean dust filters to prevent airflow obstruction.

2. **Check and Replace Thermal Paste:**
   - Remove old thermal paste from the CPU and GPU using isopropyl alcohol.
   - Apply a fresh, pea-sized amount of high-quality thermal paste before reinstalling coolers.

3. **BIOS and Firmware Updates:**
   - Visit your motherboard manufacturer's website to download the latest BIOS

updates, which can improve stability and compatibility with new hardware.

4. **Monitor Storage Health:**
   o Use CrystalDiskInfo to check SSD health and estimated lifespan.
   o Defragment HDDs and free up storage space on SSDs for better performance.

# Upgrading Components for Future-Proofing

To keep up with evolving gaming requirements, strategic component upgrades are necessary. Here's what to prioritize:

1. **GPU Upgrade:**
   o Upgrade if you experience low frame rates or if your current GPU lacks support for technologies like ray tracing or DLSS.
   o Consider GPUs like the NVIDIA RTX 30/40 series or AMD Radeon RX

6000/7000 series for long-term performance.

2. **Storage Expansion:**
   o Move from SATA SSDs to NVMe PCIe 4.0/5.0 SSDs for faster loading times.
   o Upgrade storage capacity to accommodate larger game files.

3. **RAM Upgrade:**
   o 16GB RAM is the minimum for modern gaming, but 32GB or higher can improve multitasking and overall responsiveness.

4. **CPU Upgrade:**
   o If your CPU bottlenecks your system, upgrading to newer generations, such as AMD Ryzen 7000 or Intel 12th/13th Gen, will provide better processing power and efficiency.

## Conclusion

Maintaining and troubleshooting your gaming PC is an ongoing process that ensures longevity and optimal performance. By understanding how to diagnose issues, implementing regular maintenance, and strategically upgrading components, you can keep your rig operating at peak efficiency. Future-proofing through hardware upgrades will allow you to enjoy high-quality gaming experiences without frequent full-system replacements. By following these best practices, you can ensure that your gaming PC remains powerful and reliable for years to come.

# Chapter 8: Gaming Peripherals and Accessories

Owning a high-performance gaming PC is just one aspect of creating an engaging and immersive gaming experience. To truly maximize your setup, investing in the right peripherals and accessories is essential. These components—such as monitors, keyboards, mice, audio gear, and additional accessories—greatly impact gameplay, improving comfort, responsiveness, and overall engagement.

This chapter will guide you through selecting the best gaming peripherals and accessories to enhance your experience.

## Choosing the Ideal Gaming Monitor

A monitor plays a crucial role in shaping your visual experience, affecting immersion, clarity, and gameplay performance. Several factors should be considered when selecting the right gaming monitor, including screen size, resolution, refresh rate, response time, and panel type.

## 1. Screen Size and Resolution

The monitor's size and resolution significantly affect visual clarity and overall immersion.

- **Screen Size:** The best size depends on individual preference and desk space. A 24- to 27-inch monitor is a popular choice for many gamers, balancing size and sharpness for both 1080p and 1440p gaming. Larger screens, such as 32-inch or ultrawide displays (34–49 inches), create a more immersive experience if space allows.
- **Resolution:** The resolution impacts image sharpness and detail, with common gaming resolutions including:

- **1080p (Full HD):** Works well for 24- to 27-inch monitors and is suitable for mid-range gaming PCs.

- **1440p (Quad HD):** Offers enhanced detail and clarity compared to 1080p, making it an excellent choice for high-performance gaming.

- **4K (Ultra HD):** Delivers outstanding detail, particularly on 32-inch or larger screens, but requires a powerful graphics card to maintain high frame rates.

When choosing a resolution, ensure your GPU can support it without compromising performance, especially in demanding games.

## 2. Refresh Rate and Response Time

For smooth and fluid gameplay, particularly in fast-paced genres like first-person shooters and racing games, refresh rate and response time are key considerations.

- **Refresh Rate:** This determines how often the screen updates per second, with higher rates leading to smoother visuals. Standard gaming refresh rates include:
  - **60Hz:** Sufficient for casual gaming.
  - **144Hz:** A preferred option for competitive players, offering significantly smoother performance.
  - **240Hz and 360Hz:** Best suited for professional gamers seeking ultra-responsive gameplay, requiring a high-performance GPU.
- **Response Time:** This refers to how quickly pixels change colors. A lower response time (typically 1–3 milliseconds) reduces motion blur and ghosting, improving clarity during fast movements.

## 3. Panel Types

Different monitor panels offer varying strengths:

- **IPS (In-Plane Switching):** Provides vibrant colors and wide viewing angles, making it ideal for immersive gaming and creative work.
- **TN (Twisted Nematic):** Known for fast response times and affordability but lacks in color accuracy and viewing angles.
- **VA (Vertical Alignment):** Offers high contrast ratios and deep blacks, striking a balance between IPS and TN panels.

## 4. Additional Features

- **G-Sync and FreeSync:** These adaptive sync technologies from Nvidia and AMD help eliminate screen tearing and stuttering for a smoother experience.
- **Curved Monitors:** Particularly beneficial for ultrawide and large displays, curved screens enhance immersion by creating a more natural field of view.

# Gaming Keyboards and Mice: Essential Features

A quality keyboard and mouse can significantly impact gameplay responsiveness and comfort. These peripherals act as the bridge between the player and the game, making their selection critical.

## 1. Gaming Keyboards

Mechanical keyboards are a popular choice due to their durability and tactile feedback.

- **Mechanical vs. Membrane Keyboards:**
  - **Mechanical Keyboards:** Feature individual mechanical switches under each key, offering faster actuation and improved durability. Switch types vary (e.g., Cherry MX Red, Brown, and Blue), each with different levels of resistance and sound.
  - **Membrane Keyboards:** Use rubber domes beneath the keys, providing a

softer and quieter keystroke. While more affordable, they tend to have a shorter lifespan and slower response time.

- **Key Features to Consider:**
  - ○ **Anti-Ghosting and N-Key Rollover:** Prevent missed or unregistered key presses when multiple keys are pressed at once.
  - ○ **RGB Lighting:** Customizable backlighting enhances aesthetics and can sync with in-game events.
  - ○ **Media Controls:** Dedicated buttons for volume and playback adjustments provide added convenience.

Popular mechanical keyboards include the Corsair K95 RGB Platinum, Razer Huntsman Elite, and Logitech G Pro X.

## 2. Gaming Mice

A high-performance gaming mouse enhances precision and responsiveness.

- **DPI (Dots Per Inch):** Determines mouse sensitivity, with adjustable settings allowing customization for different gaming styles.
  - **400–800 DPI:** Ideal for FPS games requiring precise aiming.
  - **1600+ DPI:** Better suited for fast-paced action or real-time strategy games.
- **Polling Rate:** The frequency at which the mouse reports its position to the PC, with higher rates (e.g., 1000Hz) improving responsiveness.
- **Ergonomics:** Comfort is vital for extended gaming sessions. Choose a mouse suited to your grip style (palm, claw, or fingertip).
- **Customizable Buttons:** Useful for MMO and MOBA games, programmable buttons provide quick access to key actions.

Notable gaming mice include the Logitech G Pro X Superlight, Razer DeathAdder Elite, and SteelSeries Rival 600.

## Audio Solutions: Headsets vs. Speakers

Quality audio enhances immersion and gameplay awareness. Whether using a headset for private gaming or speakers for a broader soundstage, the right choice depends on personal preference and gaming needs.

### 1. Gaming Headsets

Headsets combine audio output and a microphone for seamless communication in multiplayer games.

- **Sound Quality:** High-quality drivers (40mm–50mm) provide crisp and immersive sound. Virtual surround sound (e.g., 7.1) further enhances spatial awareness.
- **Microphone Quality:** A noise-canceling mic ensures clear communication with teammates.

- **Comfort:** Adjustable headbands, cushioned ear cups, and breathable materials prevent discomfort during long sessions.

Top-rated gaming headsets include the SteelSeries Arctis Pro, HyperX Cloud II, and Logitech G Pro X.

**2. Gaming Speakers**

For those who prefer open sound, gaming speakers offer a powerful alternative to headsets.

- **Stereo vs. Surround Sound:** A 2.1 system includes two speakers and a subwoofer, while 5.1 and 7.1 setups provide surround sound for deeper immersion.
- **Wired vs. Wireless:** Wired options typically offer better sound quality, while wireless systems provide convenience and less clutter.

## Additional Gaming Accessories

Beyond the essentials, other accessories can further refine the gaming experience:

- **Mouse Pads:** A high-quality surface enhances precision and consistency. Extended mouse mats accommodate both the keyboard and mouse.
- **Controllers:** For console-style gaming, controllers like the Xbox Wireless Controller or PlayStation DualSense add comfort and precision.
- **Gaming Chairs:** Ergonomic chairs with lumbar support and adjustable armrests ensure long-term comfort. Brands like Secretlab and Herman Miller excel in this area.
- **Streaming Equipment:** If you're into content creation, a stream deck allows for efficient control of stream overlays and media.

## Conclusion

Selecting the right gaming peripherals and accessories enhances your gaming experience by improving responsiveness, comfort, and immersion. By carefully considering your gaming needs and setup, you can create an optimized environment that enhances both casual and competitive gameplay. The right investment in peripherals ensures a deeper connection to the gaming world, allowing you to perform at your best while enjoying every moment.

# Chapter 9: Staying Informed and Connected

The world of gaming is an ever-evolving landscape, constantly shaped by technological innovations, industry trends, and new game releases. Whether you are a casual player or a dedicated gamer, staying informed and connected with the gaming community can significantly enhance your experience.

The ability to engage with other gamers, follow industry updates, and utilize resources for continuous learning allows you to refine your skills, discover new games, and stay ahead in the competitive gaming environment.

In this chapter, we will explore various ways to remain actively involved in the gaming community, stay up to date with industry developments, and make the most of educational resources to improve both your knowledge and gameplay.

## Engaging with the Gaming Community

Gaming has transformed into a social and interactive experience, with millions of players worldwide forming an extensive network of communities. Whether you prefer multiplayer games or enjoy single-player adventures, engaging with fellow gamers can make your gaming journey more rewarding. Here are some effective ways to stay involved:

### 1. Becoming a Part of Online Forums and Gaming Communities

Gaming forums and online communities serve as vital platforms for discussions, knowledge-sharing, and discovering new trends. These platforms connect players with similar interests and offer opportunities to exchange insights, ask questions, and get recommendations for new games.

- **Reddit:** Subreddits like r/gaming, r/pcgaming, and r/games are excellent sources of gaming news, reviews, and discussions. Many gamers use Reddit to seek troubleshooting help, share experiences, and discuss upcoming titles.

- **NeoGAF:** This community features in-depth discussions on industry trends, gaming culture, and game releases, making it a great place for serious gamers.

- **GameFAQs:** Known for its extensive game guides and walkthroughs, GameFAQs is an invaluable resource for both new and seasoned players seeking tips, strategies, and technical assistance.

Actively participating in these communities enables you to stay updated, uncover hidden gems, and receive tailored game suggestions from other gamers with similar interests.

## 2. Following Game Developers and Industry Influencers

Social media has become an essential tool for staying connected with the gaming world. Game developers, publishers, and industry influencers frequently share updates, insights, and behind-the-scenes content through their social media platforms.

Some notable accounts to follow include:

- **@PlayStation and @Xbox** – Stay informed about the latest releases, updates, and exclusive deals from these major gaming platforms.

- **@BethesdaStudios and @Naughty_Dog** – Gain insights into upcoming projects, developer interviews, and exclusive teasers from renowned studios.

- **@IGN and @GameSpot** – Follow leading gaming media outlets for comprehensive news coverage, reviews, and feature articles.

Engaging with these platforms allows you to interact with developers, participate in discussions, and stay ahead of new developments in the gaming world.

## 3. Engaging in Online Multiplayer Games

Multiplayer games provide one of the most immersive ways to connect with the gaming community. Whether through cooperative missions or competitive play, engaging in online games helps build friendships, sharpen skills, and foster teamwork.

Popular multiplayer games include:

- **Fortnite** – A battle royale game where players team up, strategize, and compete against others worldwide.

- **Call of Duty: Warzone** – Known for its fast-paced action and team-based gameplay, this title offers an intense competitive experience.

- **Valorant** – A tactical shooter requiring precise strategy and teamwork to succeed.

- **World of Warcraft** – One of the longest-running MMORPGs, offering vast in-game communities and cooperative experiences.

Many games feature built-in voice chat and external platforms like Discord, where players can interact, form teams, and discuss strategies.

## 4. Creating and Sharing Gaming Content

For those passionate about gaming, content creation is an excellent way to contribute to the community. Sharing gameplay videos, tutorials, reviews, or creative game-related content can help build an audience and foster engagement.

Ways to share gaming content:

- **YouTube and Twitch:** Streaming gameplay, reviewing new releases, or providing in-depth game analysis can establish you as a credible voice in the gaming world.

- **TikTok and Instagram:** Short-form gaming clips, memes, and highlights can quickly gain traction and connect you with a wider audience.

- **Game Modding:** Contributing mods to games like Skyrim, Fallout, or Minecraft adds new features and enhances the experience for others in the community.

Even if content creation isn't your focus, supporting fellow creators through likes, comments, and shares helps keep the community thriving.

## Keeping Up with Industry Trends

With constant advancements in gaming technology and frequent game releases, keeping up with industry trends ensures you stay informed and ahead of the curve.

# 1. Tracking Game Releases and Industry News

Hundreds of new games are released annually, ranging from indie gems to AAA blockbusters. To avoid missing out on titles that match your interests, consider these sources:

- **Gaming News Websites:** Platforms like IGN, Kotaku, and Polygon provide daily updates on upcoming releases, reviews, and industry insights.

- **Game Platforms:** Stores like Steam, Epic Games Store, and PlayStation Store feature "Coming Soon" sections to help track upcoming games.

- **Developer Newsletters:** Many game developers offer newsletters with exclusive insights, release announcements, and behind-the-scenes content.

## 2. Understanding Technological Advancements

As gaming technology advances, staying informed about the latest hardware and software developments can enhance your gaming experience.

- **Virtual Reality (VR):** Headsets like Oculus Quest 2 and PlayStation VR2 are revolutionizing immersive gaming.

- **Ray Tracing:** Graphics improvements with ray tracing create more realistic lighting effects in games.

- **Cloud Gaming:** Services like Xbox Cloud Gaming and GeForce Now enable gaming without high-end hardware.

Following tech websites, watching hardware reviews, and reading industry blogs can help you make informed decisions about gaming hardware and software.

## 3. Attending Gaming Events and Conferences

Major gaming conventions showcase upcoming releases, industry innovations, and exclusive developer insights. Some notable events include:

- **E3 (Electronic Entertainment Expo)** – A premier event where leading developers unveil new games and technologies.

- **Gamescom** – One of the largest gaming trade fairs, featuring announcements and developer interviews.

- **The Game Awards** – An annual event celebrating gaming achievements while featuring world premieres and major announcements.

Even if you can't attend in person, many of these events are streamed live, providing valuable insights into the gaming industry's future.

# Resources for Continuous Learning in Gaming

Beyond playing games, continuously learning about game mechanics, strategies, and development can enhance your overall gaming experience.

## 1. Online Courses and Tutorials

Platforms like Udemy and Coursera offer courses in game design, programming, and strategy guides for competitive games. YouTube channels such as Game Maker's Toolkit and Extra Credits provide valuable insights into game mechanics and design principles.

## 2. Podcasts and Webinars

Listening to gaming podcasts is a great way to stay updated while on the go. Popular podcasts include:

- **Kinda Funny Games Daily** – Covers daily gaming news and trends.

- **The Giant Bombcast** – Features discussions on video games, industry developments, and gaming culture.

## 3. Participating in Online Learning Communities

Engaging in gaming-focused subreddits, Discord groups, and game development forums allows you to exchange knowledge, ask questions, and refine your gaming skills.

## Conclusion

Staying connected in the gaming world goes beyond just playing games. By actively engaging with the community, keeping up with industry trends, and continuously learning, you can enrich your gaming experience. Whether participating in discussions, tracking game releases, or exploring new technologies, the gaming world offers endless opportunities for growth and engagement. With the right resources and community involvement, you can elevate your passion for gaming and stay ahead in this dynamic and ever-evolving industry.

# Additional Tips

## 1. Hardware Comparisons & Buying Tips

### Processor (CPU):

- **AMD Ryzen 9 9950X3D:** Released on March 12, 2025, this processor boasts 16 Zen 5 cores with second-generation 3D V-Cache technology, offering a base clock speed of 4.3 GHz and a boost up to 5.7 GHz. It's optimized for both gaming and productivity tasks, making it a top choice for high-end gaming rigs.

- **Intel Core i9-14900K:** Intel's flagship processor features high core counts and clock speeds, delivering exceptional performance for gaming and multitasking.

### Graphics Card (GPU):

- **NVIDIA GeForce RTX 5070 Ti:** This GPU offers significant performance improvements over previous generations, supporting real-time ray tracing and DLSS 3.5 technology. It's ideal for gamers seeking high frame rates at 1440p and 4K resolutions.

- **AMD Radeon RX 7900 XTX:** With 24GB of GDDR6 memory and support for FSR 3.0, this GPU provides excellent performance for high-resolution gaming.

## RAM & Storage:

- **DDR5 vs. DDR6:** While DDR5 RAM is prevalent, DDR6 is emerging with higher speeds and lower latencies, offering improved performance for gaming applications.

- **Storage Solutions:** PCIe 5.0 NVMe SSDs provide faster data transfer rates, reducing game load times and improving overall system responsiveness

## Cooling Systems:

- **Air Cooling vs. Liquid Cooling:** Air coolers like the Noctua NH-D15 offer reliable performance, while AIO liquid coolers provide enhanced cooling efficiency, essential for overclocked systems.

## Power Supply (PSU):

- **Wattage and Efficiency:** Selecting a PSU with adequate wattage and an 80+ Gold or Platinum efficiency rating ensures stable power delivery and system reliability.

## 2. Game-Specific Hardware Recommendations

### Esports & Competitive Games:

- **Optimal Specs:** For titles like "Valorant" and "Counter-Strike 2," a high-refresh-rate monitor paired with a GPU like the RTX 4070 Super ensures smooth gameplay.

### AAA Open-World Games:

- **Ray Tracing Performance:** Games such as "Cyberpunk 2077" benefit from GPUs with robust ray tracing capabilities, like the RTX 5070 Ti, to enhance visual fidelity.

**VR & Streaming:**

- **System Requirements:** A powerful CPU and GPU combination is crucial for VR gaming and streaming, ensuring low latency and high-quality visuals.

## 3. Optimizing Your Gaming PC

**Overclocking Tips:**

- **Safe Practices:** Utilize motherboard BIOS settings to adjust CPU multipliers and voltages carefully, ensuring system stability during overclocking.

**BIOS Settings for Gamers:**

- **XMP Profiles:** Enable XMP (Extreme Memory Profile) to allow RAM to run at its rated speed, enhancing system performance.

**Cooling & Airflow Optimization:**

- **Fan Placement:** Strategically position intake and exhaust fans to maintain optimal airflow, reducing component temperatures.

## Cable Management:

- **Improving Airflow:** Organize cables using tie-downs and routing channels to prevent airflow obstruction, aiding in better cooling.

## 4. Future-Proofing Your Build

## Upgrade Path for 2026 & Beyond:

- **Component Selection:** Choose a motherboard with PCIe 5.0 support and ample expansion slots to accommodate future hardware upgrades.

## AI-Integrated GPUs:

- **Advancements:** AI technologies like NVIDIA's DLSS 3.5 enhance gaming performance by utilizing AI-driven upscaling and rendering techniques.

### PCIe 5.0 & DDR6 RAM Adoption:

- **Performance Benefits:** Adopting PCIe 5.0 and DDR6 RAM provides higher data transfer rates and memory speeds, essential for future gaming applications.

### Quantum Dot & OLED Monitors:

- **Display Technologies:** These monitors offer superior color accuracy and contrast ratios, enhancing the visual gaming experience.

### 5. Troubleshooting & Common Mistakes

### Common PC Build Errors:

- **Component Compatibility:** Ensure all components are compatible to prevent issues during assembly and operation.

### Blue Screen of Death (BSOD) Fixes:

- **Diagnostic Steps:** Use tools like Windows Memory Diagnostic to identify and resolve hardware-related BSOD errors.

**Performance Drops & Bottlenecks:**

- **Identifying Issues:** Monitor system performance to detect bottlenecks, allowing targeted upgrades for optimal performance.

## 6. Gaming Accessories & Peripherals

**Best Monitors for 2025:**

- **High Refresh Rates:** Monitors with 144Hz or higher refresh rates provide smoother visuals, beneficial for fast-paced gaming.

## Mechanical Keyboards vs. Membrane:

- **Gaming Performance:** Mechanical keyboards offer tactile feedback and durability, enhancing the gaming experience.

## Wireless vs. Wired Mouse:

- **Latency Considerations:** Modern wireless mice offer low latency comparable to wired versions, providing flexibility without compromising performance.

**Gaming Chairs & Desks:**

- **Ergonomics:** Investing in ergonomic chairs and adjustable desks promotes comfort during extended gaming sessions.

## 7. Software & Security for Gamers

**Best Antivirus & VPN for Gamers:**

- **Surfshark One:** This comprehensive security suite offers real-time protection with a lightweight cloud antivirus engine, ensuring minimal impact on gaming performance. It includes a robust VPN with unlimited connections, utilizing military-grade 256-bit encryption to safeguard against DDoS attacks and maintain privacy. Features like split tunneling allow gamers to route specific traffic through the VPN, optimizing both security and speed.

- **Norton 360 for Gamers:** Tailored specifically for gaming enthusiasts, this suite provides real-time threat protection, a secure VPN, and a dedicated gaming mode that minimizes interruptions by suppressing notifications during gameplay. It also offers dark web monitoring for gamertags and personal information, ensuring comprehensive security.

- **Bitdefender Total Security:** Known for its high detection rates and minimal system impact, Bitdefender offers real-time data protection, advanced threat defense, and a VPN. The VPN, powered by Hotspot Shield's infrastructure, provides high-speed connections suitable for streaming and gaming, with over 4,000 servers across 53 countries. However, the standard version includes a daily data cap of 200MB, with an option to upgrade for unlimited data.

**Windows 11 Gaming Mode Optimization:**

Windows 11 introduces features like DirectStorage and Auto HDR, enhancing gaming performance and visuals. DirectStorage reduces game load times by optimizing data transfer between the storage device and GPU, while Auto HDR enhances the visual experience of older titles by automatically upgrading standard dynamic range content to high dynamic range. To optimize performance, gamers can enable the built-in Game Mode, which prioritizes gaming processes and minimizes background activity.

**However,** certain security features like Memory Integrity and Virtual Machine Platform (VMP) may impact performance. Users can choose to disable these features temporarily during gaming sessions for optimal performance, but should be aware of the potential security implications.

**Overlays & FPS Counters:**

- **MSI Afterburner:** A popular tool among gamers, MSI Afterburner provides real-time monitoring of system performance, including

GPU temperature, usage, and frame rates. It also offers overclocking capabilities, allowing users to fine-tune their hardware for optimal performance.

- **NVIDIA GeForce Experience:** This software suite offers features like ShadowPlay for recording gameplay, Ansel for in-game photography, and an overlay that displays real-time performance metrics, including FPS. It also provides game-ready drivers and optimal game settings tailored to the user's hardware.

## 8. Building a Budget vs. High-End PC

**$1000 Gaming Build:**

- **CPU:** AMD Ryzen 5 5600X – A 6-core processor offering strong performance for gaming and multitasking.

- **GPU:** NVIDIA GeForce RTX 3060 – Provides excellent 1080p performance with ray tracing capabilities.

- **RAM:** 16GB DDR4 at 3200MHz – Ensures smooth multitasking and gaming performance.

- **Storage:** 500GB NVMe SSD – Fast load times and quick system responsiveness.

- **Motherboard:** B550 chipset motherboard – Offers PCIe 4.0 support and future upgrade paths.

- **PSU:** 650W 80+ Bronze certified – Reliable power delivery with room for future upgrades.

## $2500+ High-End Build:

- **CPU:** Intel Core i9-12900K – A 16-core processor delivering top-tier performance for gaming and content creation.

- **GPU:** NVIDIA GeForce RTX 4090 – Exceptional performance for 4K gaming with advanced ray tracing.

- **RAM:** 32GB DDR5 at 5200MHz – High-speed memory for demanding applications.

- **Storage:** 1TB PCIe 4.0 NVMe SSD – Ultra-fast storage for quick load times and data transfer.

- **Motherboard:** Z690 chipset motherboard – Supports the latest CPU and memory technologies with robust power delivery.

- **PSU:** 850W 80+ Gold certified – Ensures stable power for high-end components.

**Best Prebuilt Gaming PCs:**

- **Alienware Aurora R13:** Known for its sleek design and powerful components, the Aurora R13 offers configurations with the latest Intel processors and NVIDIA RTX 30-series GPUs. It also features advanced cooling solutions and customizable RGB lighting.

- **HP Omen 45L:** This prebuilt system provides high-end performance with options for AMD Ryzen 9 processors and NVIDIA RTX 3080 Ti GPUs. Its tool-less design allows for easy upgrades, and the Omen Gaming Hub software offers system optimization and customization.

- **Corsair Vengeance i7200:** Combining Corsair's quality components with powerful performance, the Vengeance i7200 offers Intel Core i9 processors and NVIDIA RTX 3090 GPUs. It also includes Corsair's iCUE software for system monitoring and RGB lighting control.

# Appendices

## A. Glossary of Gaming PC Terms

Understanding gaming PC terminology is crucial for both beginners and experienced gamers. Here's a glossary of essential terms you should know:

### Hardware Terms

- **CPU (Central Processing Unit):** The "brain" of the computer, responsible for executing instructions and processing tasks. High-performance CPUs improve gaming speed and responsiveness.

- **GPU (Graphics Processing Unit):** Also known as a graphics card, it renders visuals in games. The better the GPU, the smoother and more detailed the graphics.

- **RAM (Random Access Memory):** Temporary memory that helps your system run games and applications. More RAM allows for better multitasking and performance.

- **SSD (Solid State Drive):** A fast storage device that significantly reduces load times compared to traditional HDDs.

- **HDD (Hard Disk Drive):** A traditional storage device that is slower but offers more capacity for storing games and media.

- **VRAM (Video RAM):** Dedicated memory on the GPU used for rendering graphics, textures, and images in games.

- **Power Supply Unit (PSU):** Converts electricity from an outlet into power that your computer components can use. A high-quality PSU ensures stable power delivery.

- **Cooling System:** Includes fans, liquid cooling, and heat sinks to prevent overheating in gaming PCs.

## Software and Gaming Terms

- **FPS (Frames Per Second):** The number of frames a game renders per second. Higher FPS results in smoother gameplay.

- **Refresh Rate:** Measured in Hz, it indicates how many times the monitor updates per second. A 144Hz monitor offers smoother visuals than a 60Hz one.

- **Overclocking:** The process of increasing a component's clock speed (CPU/GPU) to enhance performance, often requiring additional cooling.

- **Anti-Aliasing:** A graphics setting that smooths jagged edges in-game for a cleaner look.

- **V-Sync (Vertical Sync):** A setting that prevents screen tearing by synchronizing frame rates with the monitor's refresh rate.

- **Ray Tracing:** Advanced lighting and shadow rendering technology for realistic graphics.

- **Ping:** The response time between your system and the game server, measured in milliseconds.

Lower ping results in better online gaming performance.

- **Latency:** The delay between input (pressing a key or mouse click) and the corresponding action appearing on-screen.

## B. Recommended Tools and Software

For an optimal gaming experience, having the right tools and software is essential. Here's a list of must-have programs:

### System Performance and Monitoring

- **MSI Afterburner:** A powerful tool for overclocking GPUs and monitoring system performance.
- **HWMonitor:** Tracks system temperatures, fan speeds, and power consumption.
- **CPU-Z and GPU-Z:** Provide detailed information about your CPU and GPU specifications.

## Gaming Optimization

- **Razer Cortex:** Boosts system performance by allocating more resources to games.
- **NVIDIA GeForce Experience / AMD Radeon Software:** Optimize game settings and update GPU drivers for better performance.
- **Windows Game Mode:** Built-in Windows feature that improves gaming performance by limiting background processes.

## Communication and Streaming

- **Discord:** A popular communication platform for gamers, featuring voice and text chat.
- **OBS Studio:** A free tool for live streaming and recording gameplay.
- **Steam Chat:** A built-in chat system for Steam users to communicate while gaming.

## Game Management and Mods

- **Steam and Epic Games Launcher:** Platforms for purchasing, managing, and launching games.
- **Mod Organizer 2:** Essential for managing mods in games like Skyrim and Fallout.
- **Nexus Mod Manager:** A popular tool for installing and organizing game modifications.

## Security and Maintenance

- **Malwarebytes:** Protects against gaming-related malware and phishing attempts.
- **CCleaner:** Clears temporary files and optimizes system performance.
- **Driver Booster:** Ensures your system drivers are always up to date.

## C. Resource List: Websites, Forums, and Communities

Staying informed and connected with the gaming community can enhance your experience. Below is a categorized list of useful resources:

## Gaming News and Reviews

- **IGN (ign.com):** Covers gaming news, reviews, and upcoming releases.
- **GameSpot (gamespot.com):** Provides in-depth reviews, trailers, and industry insights.
- **Kotaku (kotaku.com):** Features gaming news, controversies, and opinions.

## Gaming Forums and Discussion Platforms

- **Reddit (reddit.com/r/gaming, r/pcgaming, r/gamedev):** A hub for gamers to discuss games, hardware, and industry news.
- **NeoGAF (neogaf.com):** A discussion forum for gaming news and community engagement.
- **GameFAQs (gamefaqs.com):** Provides game walkthroughs, FAQs, and a dedicated gaming forum.

## Gaming Communities and Multiplayer Connections

- **Discord (discord.com):** Home to thousands of gaming servers for different communities.
- **Twitch (twitch.tv):** A live streaming platform where gamers can watch and interact with streamers.
- **Steam Community (steamcommunity.com):** Forums, guides, and group chats for Steam users.

## Game Development and Modding

- **Unity (unity.com):** A leading game engine for indie and professional developers.
- **Unreal Engine (unrealengine.com):** A powerful game engine used by AAA developers.
- **Nexus Mods (nexusmods.com):** The best place to find and download mods for various PC games.

## PC Hardware and Troubleshooting

- **Tom's Hardware (tomshardware.com):** Guides on building and upgrading gaming PCs.
- **PCPartPicker (pcpartpicker.com):** Helps you choose compatible PC components.
- **Linus Tech Tips (linustechtips.com):** A tech website and YouTube channel with gaming PC tutorials.

## D. Troubleshooting Flowchart

If you're experiencing issues with your gaming PC, follow this step-by-step troubleshooting guide:

### Step 1: Identify the Problem

Is your PC turning on?

- **No:** Check power supply connections, try a different outlet, and verify that the PSU is functioning.
- **Yes:** Proceed to Step 2.

### Step 2: Boot Issues

Does your PC boot to Windows?

- **No:** Check for error messages, try booting into Safe Mode, and reseat RAM and GPU.
- **Yes:** Proceed to Step 3.

## Step 3: Game Crashes or Lag

Is your game crashing, freezing, or running slowly?

- **Yes:** Check for overheating, update GPU drivers, and adjust in-game settings.
- **No:** Proceed to Step 4.

## Step 4: Internet or Multiplayer Issues

Experiencing lag or disconnections in online games?

- **Yes:** Test internet speed, restart router, and check for background downloads.
- **No:** Proceed to Step 5.

## Step 5: Hardware Issues

Are you hearing strange noises or experiencing sudden shutdowns?

- **Yes:** Check for overheating, clean fans, and test PSU stability.
- **No:** Contact customer support or seek professional repair.

Following this flowchart will help diagnose and fix common gaming PC issues efficiently.